CHECKERBOARD SOCIAL STUDIES LIBRARY

CHARACTER COUNTS

GOOD CITIZENSHIP COUNTS

by Marie Bender

Reviewed by
Dr. Howard Kirschenbaum, Ed.D.

ABDO Publishing Company

visit us at
www.abdopub.com

Published by ABDO Publishing Company, 4940 Viking Drive, Edina, Minnesota 55435. Copyright © 2003 by Abdo Consulting Group, Inc. International copyrights reserved in all countries. No part of this book may be reproduced in any form without written permission from the publisher.

Printed in the United States.

Photo credits: Comstock, Corbis Images, Corel, Diamar, Eyewire Images, Image 100, Frédéric Cirou/PhotoAlto, PhotoDisc, Skjold Photography

Editors: Kate A. Conley, Stephanie Hedlund

Design and production: Mighty Media

Library of Congress Cataloging-in-Publication Data

Bender, Marie, 1968-
    Good citizenship counts / Marie Bender.
      p. cm. -- (Character counts)
    Includes index.
    Summary: Defines citizenship and discusses how to demonstrate this responsibility at home, with friends, at school, in the community, and with respect to government.
    ISBN 1-57765-871-X
    1. Citizenship--Juvenile literature. [1. Citizenship.] I. Title.

JF801 .B455 2002
323.6--dc21

           2002074670

Internationally known educator and author Howard Kirschenbaum has worked with schools, non-profit organizations, governmental agencies, and private businesses around the world to develop school/family/community relations and values education programs for more than 30 years. He has written more than 20 books about character education, including a high school curriculum. Dr. Kirschenbaum is currently the Frontier Professor of School, Family, and Community Relations at the University of Rochester and teaches classes in counseling and human development.

Contents

CHARACTER COUNTS

Character is much easier kept than recovered.

—*Thomas Paine, political theorist and writer*

Your character is the combination of **traits** that makes you an individual. It's not your physical traits, such as the color of your eyes or how tall you are. Rather, character is your thoughts, feelings, beliefs, and values.

Your character shows in the way you interact with your family, friends, teachers, and other community members. People who are well liked and successful are said to have a good character. Many traits build good character. Some of these traits include caring, fairness, honesty, good citizenship, responsibility, and respect.

Good Citizenship Counts

Bobby's neighbor got a new dog. Bobby soon noticed that the neighbor didn't take very good care of the dog. He hit the dog and didn't give it enough food or water. The dog was also left outside all of the time, without any kind of shelter to protect it from the rain or the hot sun.

Bobby told his mother and stepfather that he was worried about the dog. So they called the Humane Society. It sent a worker to the neighbor's house to check on the dog's living conditions.

The Humane Society took the dog away from Bobby's neighbor and cared for it at the shelter until a kinder owner adopted it. Bobby was happy the Humane Society saved the dog. It inspired him to volunteer at the shelter. There, he cared for and played with the animals.

Bobby made good citizenship count.

WHAT IS GOOD CITIZENSHIP?

*Citizenship is man's basic right for it is nothing less than
the right to have rights . . .*

—*Earl Warren, chief justice of the U.S. Supreme Court*

As citizens, people who live in a community, city, state, or country have certain **rights** and responsibilities. Good citizens know their rights and understand their responsibilities. Good citizens actively participate in matters that are important to themselves, as well as to their family, friends, neighbors, community, and country.

GOOD CITIZENSHIP

As a citizen living in a **democracy**, you have many **rights**. But rights also come with responsibilities. For example, you have the right to have your own beliefs. However, you also have the responsibility to respect the rights of other people. You have the right to express your opinions. But you also have the responsibility to listen to other people's opinions. You have the right to say "no" if a friend asks you to do something you disagree with. You also have the responsibility to accept a friend saying "no" to you. You have the right to make your own choices and the responsibility to accept the **consequences** of those choices.

There is no specific right or wrong way to practice good citizenship. That's because each person serves other people or causes in the way he or she thinks is best.

There are many ways to be a good citizen. When you help and serve others, you show that you are a good citizen and leader. Other people will look to you to share ideas that will make your community a better place to live.

Good citizens show respect for the rights of other people. They stand up for themselves and others. They get involved in activities that help people, animals, and the environment.

Think about it...

What are your rights as a citizen?

What are your responsibilities?

Responsible citizens follow the rules in their families and schools. They follow the laws in their communities and countries. These efforts maintain a peaceful, clean, and safe place to live.

GOOD CITIZENSHIP

GOOD CITIZENSHIP AND FAMILY

The future depends entirely on what each of us does every day.

—*Gloria Steinem, feminist*

Y ou can practice good citizenship with your family. Being a good citizen means that you show respect for others, participate in activities and decision-making, and help family members. You have **rights** and responsibilities that make living with your family peaceful. When you learn and **demonstrate** good citizenship at home, it will be easier to use these skills with your friends, at your school, and in your community.

You can follow your parents' rules to show you are a good citizen within your family. It shows you

11

respect your parents' authority and are willing to do what they ask you to do. Sometimes, you may disagree with their decisions. You have the **right** to talk with them about their decisions in a respectful manner.

Does your family have meetings?

How does it or would it help in your family?

Have your parents ever followed one of your suggestions?

How would you change the rules and responsibilities in your family?

Many families have meetings to talk about rules and responsibilities. The meetings also give family members a chance to ask questions and share their feelings. It is important to participate in family meetings. This is a time to talk openly about your ideas and opinions. If you do not have family meetings, you can ask your parents if you could start having them.

Helping family members shows you are a good citizen. When family members learn to work together, they can accomplish things that benefit everyone. Cooking, cleaning, laundry, shopping, and yard work are chores family members can share to help each other.

Being a good citizen at home means you do things without being asked. For instance, if your younger **siblings** are having trouble with their homework, you could offer to help them. You could take the dog for a walk, clean up the kitchen after dinner, or pick up your room before being asked to. When you do things without being asked, you are helping others and showing you are responsible and caring.

Think about it...

What are some ways you can show you are a good citizen at home?

Things to Do for Your Family Without Being Asked

 Take care of family pets.

 Do your homework.

 Return library books.

 Make your own lunch.

Fold the clean clothes.

Sweep the floor.

Do the dishes.

Play with your siblings.

Talk to your parents.

 Make a card for someone who is sick.

Call your grandparents.

Empty the trash.

Walk your younger siblings home from school.

14

GOOD CITIZENSHIP AND FRIEN.

The true test of civilization is not the census, nor the size of the cities, nor the crops—no, but the kind of man the country turns out. —Ralph Waldo Emerson, poet and essayist

Being a good citizen with your friends basically means being a good friend. This means you care about your friends and want them to be happy. To do this, you can listen to your friends and try to help them with their problems. You can respect your friends' opinions, beliefs, feelings, and decisions. You can also stand up for your friends if they are being teased.

Being a good friend also involves **compromise**. You may not always

agree with your friends. It is important to respect others and their **rights**. However, you have the responsibility to be true to yourself.

It is okay to disagree with some things your friends think or do. Disagreeing in a respectful manner shows good citizenship and true friendship. If your friend wants to do something that is wrong, such as stealing, being a good citizen means trying to talk him or her out of it. If you can't change your friend's mind, then good citizenship means not going along.

Good citizens try to meet new people and make new friends. Over time, you and your friends grow and change, and so do your opinions. So it is important to be open to making new friends. A good way to meet new people is to join clubs or teams. You can also volunteer at organizations where you can meet other people who share your interests. When you involve yourself in new experiences, you may realize you have more in common with others than you thought.

Think about it...

When was the last time you made a new friend?

Is it hard to make new friends? Where do you meet new people?

GOOD CITIZENSHIP AND SCHOOL

One has the right to be wrong in a democracy.

—Claude Pepper, political leader

Your school is a community. The students, teachers, and other staff members are citizens of your school. Being a good citizen at school means you follow the rules, respect the **rights** of others, and help classmates and teachers. A good citizen is also committed to doing his or her

best every day. Teachers and students rely on the leadership of good citizens within the school to create a positive place to learn.

Good citizens are friendly. They reach out to new students to get to know them, help them make friends, and learn about the school. Good citizens stand up for their classmates if they see others picking on them. They speak up when others are being unfair or hurting someone else's feelings. And good citizens stand up for their own beliefs, opinions, and values even if others disagree.

Have you ever stood up for someone who was being bullied? How did you feel?

Has anyone ever stood up for you? How did it make you feel?

You can also be a good citizen at school by joining school activities and organizations. Attending athletic events such as football, basketball, soccer, tennis, or hockey games shows you have school spirit. Some schools have other activities such as chess club, math club, computer club, or language clubs. These activities provide students with a chance to meet others who have similar interests.

Many schools also have a student government. Students elect class presidents and other officers. You can participate by voting in the elections, helping one of the candidates campaign, or even running for an office.

Other student organizations help in the community by doing service projects. Projects may include picking up litter, tutoring younger students, feeding homeless people, visiting nursing homes, collecting baby clothes or items for a women's shelter, sponsoring a family during holidays, or planting gardens in parks. These are good ways to be involved in your school and to be a good citizen.

Think about it...

What school organizations do you belong to?

What activities would you like to participate in if your school offered them?

Can you think of other ways you can show good citizenship at school?

GOOD CITIZENSHIP AND COMMUNITY

Ask not what your country can do for you, but what you can do for your country.

—John F. Kennedy, thirty-fifth president of the United States

Being a good citizen in your community means obeying its laws, treating neighbors respectfully, and helping others. You can do this by helping a neighbor with yard work, shoveling snow, raking leaves, or emptying the trash. Sometimes, just talking to your neighbors shows you care about and respect them.

You can also be a good citizen by getting involved in organizations and youth groups that volunteer in the community. These groups often organize food and clothing drives, after-school tutoring and childcare, or neighborhood cleanup days.

Think about it…

What are some things around your neighborhood that need attention?

What can you do about these things?

Another way to be a good citizen is to make **donations**. You can give clothes you have outgrown to organizations that distribute them to people in need. You can collect canned foods for your local food shelf. You can save part of your allowance to give to others. You can donate one of your birthday presents to a foster care program.

Good citizens also help take care of the environment. There are many ways you can help create a clean and safe place to live. You can **recycle** cans, bottles, and paper to reduce waste. You can pick up litter in the park to show you respect public property. You can feed the birds to show you care about and respect animals. You can use **organic** household cleaners and keep harmful chemicals out of the water and air to protect the environment.

Watching out and speaking up are also ways to be a good citizen. When a neighbor is on vacation, you can show you are a good citizen by looking out for any unusual activity. If you see something in your neighborhood that needs to be fixed, such as unsafe playground equipment or uneven sidewalks, you can tell your parents or another adult. Adults can help you learn how to make positive changes in your community. When you care enough to get involved, others will follow your lead.

GOOD CITIZENSHIP AND YOU

This country has more problems than it should tolerate and more solutions than it uses.

—*Ralph Nader, lawyer, writer, and politician*

There are many big problems in the world, including hunger, homelessness, disease, pollution, and violence. Sometimes thinking about how to make a difference can be overwhelming. To be a good citizen, you don't have to solve all of the world's problems, or even try to. You only need to pick a few things you can do to help.

It is easier to make a difference if you choose things that fit with interests you already have. If you like to spend time at the community center, then you can take a few minutes each time you go there to pick up litter. If you are good at schoolwork, you can volunteer to tutor younger students. If you like nature, you can help plant gardens in the park. If you like to

Think about it...

What did you do this week that shows good citizenship?

Can you think of a service project that you would like to be involved in?

cook, you can volunteer at a soup kitchen. If you look, you will likely find at least one organization that serves the community in ways that are interesting to you.

GOOD CITIZENSHIP AND GOVERNMENT

Let us at all times remember that all American citizens are brothers of a common country, and should dwell together in bonds of fraternal feeling.

—Abraham Lincoln, sixteenth president of the United States

Learning about and getting involved in the government in your city, state, and country are important ways to be a good citizen. In a **democracy**, citizens choose leaders who make laws based on the opinions of the people.

Democracy works best if people let their leaders know what they want. Citizens can do this by voting and by writing letters to lawmakers. As a student, you can learn how the government works. You can talk to your parents about who they vote for and why. You can ask to go with them when they vote to see what it is like. By doing these things, you will be a well-informed citizen when you are old enough to vote.

Another way to learn about government is to attend town council meetings. This will show you how laws are made and changed. If the law

being discussed affects children, you may be asked to speak at the meeting to share your opinion. So even though you are not old enough to vote, you can still get involved. And getting involved is a big part of being a good citizen.

Showing patriotism is also a way to be a good citizen. Being patriotic means showing love for and devotion to your country. You can sing the national anthem, stand in respect of your nation's flag, and work to improve your country.

What are some ways you can get involved in the local, state, and national government?

29

Good Citizens

Many people show good citizenship. Think about people you know and what they do. Who do you consider to be good citizens?

Government officials

Law enforcement officers

Firefighters

Teachers

Volunteers

Religious leaders

Rescue workers

Missionaries

Youth leaders

Conservationists

GLOSSARY

compromise - settling an argument by having each side give up part of its demand.

consequence - something that results from an earlier action or happening; outcome.

democracy - a governmental system in which the people vote on how to run the country.

demonstrate - to make a show of; express openly.

donation - a gift.

organic - of, using, or grown without benefit of chemical fertilizers or insecticides.

recycle - to make suitable for reuse.

right - a legal or moral claim to something.

sibling - a brother or sister.

trait - a quality that distinguishes one person or group from another.

WEB SITES

Would you like to learn more about character? Please visit www.abdopub.com to find up-to-date Web site links about caring, fairness, honesty, good citizenship, responsibility, and respect. These links are routinely monitored and updated to provide the most current information available.

INDEX

For the Character Counts series, ABDO Publishing Company researched leading character education resources and references in an effort to present accurate information about developing good character and why doing so is important. While the title of the series is Character Counts, these books do not represent the Character Counts organization or its mission. ABDO Publishing Company recognizes and thanks the numerous organizations that provide information and support for building good character in school, at home, and in the community.